TIN, COLUMBITE, TANTALITE.... SOLID MINERALS MINING - RESUSCITATION FOR INVESTMENT

REVIVING TIN, COLUMBITE, TANTALITE AND ASSOCIATED SOLID MINERALS MINING IN NIGERIA AND INDEED PLATEAU STATE FOR IMPROVED IGR

DEDICATION

To the "I AM" that knows the end from the beginning –
take the Glory Jehovah God.

To these two that fulfill my joy – Glorious Keller and
Trisha Pearl.

TARGET READERS

1. Federal Government of Nigeria through the Federal ministry of Solid minerals.

2. Plateau State government through its State ministry of mines and energy.

3. All students of tertiary education in the department of Mining engineering, geology and mining and History department.

4. Independent Practicing Mining company directors and managers engage in the business of Tin, Columbite, Tantalite and other related mineral ores.

5. Professional historians, private and public Archiving institutions in Nigeria, Africa and the World.

6. Prospective local entrepreneurs', investors, retail traders wishing to engage in the business of tin,

columbite, tantalite and other related solid minerals.

7. Prospective foreign direct investors to the solid minerals sub sector in Nigeria.

8. Practicing and prospective 36 mining license holders, Tin shed Operators and artisan miners.

9. Interested local mechanical engineers, designers and fabricators in the area of mining equipments and machines hardware and spare parts re-design, fabrication and production.

10. To all members of Nigeria mining association

TABLE OF CONTENT

FORWARD

In October 2006, I went to Enugu Street Jos to see my long time friend Alex. We had not seen for the past three years. We greeted each other fondly and exchanged complements. I observed that the large house was unusually serene, devoid of the usual activities there. I then asked my friend Alex, is there no work today? Where is everybody" he then answered "well, my friend the place had been like this for some time now" "but why? I asked further. "Why? Because nothing is happening and people have deserted mining work for other endeavors" he answered.

I was taken aback not by his answer but by the time difference between when I left active mining in 2002 to this very moment. At least at that time there are still a lot of miners in business despite a sharp drop in price. Alex late father owns a lot of properties in the State; he was among the early miners from the southern part of the country that worked with the white miners.

I started mining work in the early nineties, to be precise

in 1990 at Alex father's tin shed (factory for processing tin and columbite). The tin shed occupied one big hall adjacent to four other large buildings which they owned. I had my first mining experience there. I reminisce how it started, when I gained admission into government science school kuru to start SS1, I went late and the admission was closed, so because I really wanted to go to that particular school, I decided to wait for the next secession. I had ample time then and was only eager to accept when my Barrack friends and neighbors invited me to their work. Since then, I had never looked back, in fact I have no reason to, because it kept me away from home and idleness and it took away my thought of missing school. Above all, this opportunity filled my pockets with cash. That was how I come to work at Alex father's tin shed at Enugu or Cemetery street adjacent Ola Hospital, which was then sublet to the famous miner on the Plateau-chief John Agbatutu(of blessed memory) as one of his numerous branches. In those days mining was fun, and being a new experience, one is anxious to learn it despite the tedious nature of the work involve. Every tin shed then was characterize by three things- population, machine sound and much activity. It was a hustling and bustling activity for any typical tin shed in any given day. In no time, I settle down to my new endeavor and forgot about school and idleness, rather, I focused my attention to the present reality of making earns need to help myself.

While there at the location of the old tin shed which has witnessed a lot of activities in the past, even in quick income generation; I could only but wonder what went wrong with the industry. As if by in-depth imagination, I could hear the peoples' noise intermingled with the loud machine noise and see the final product being tested and weighed.

This visit had prompted the need in me to write about the neglect of an important institution and how to revive it. This is a sector that previously generated revenue to the state and the country at large, It leads to fast growth and development of the Tin city and it employs more people (only reviled by the construction industry) in modern time than any other sector of the economy. The solid mineral industry, to which Tin and Columbite belongs, had in its credit high rate of return on investment.

CHAPTER 1:

1.0 INTRODUCTION

1.1 NIGERIA SOLID MINERAL SECTOR; HISTORICAL BACKGROUND:

Nigeria has a large land area of about 924 square kilometers with a terrain that is very variable, with Mountains in the South East, Hills and Plateaus including the Jos Plateau in the centre, lowland in the South, and plains in the North. Nigeria's climate varies from Equatorial in the South to Tropical in the Centre, and Arid in the North. Annual rainfall varies from over 4000mm in the South to less than 250mm in parts of the North, with a national average put at 1180mm. The rainfall is characterized by two seasons, the wet and the dry season.

Mining is one of the oldest economic activities in Nigeria dating back to prehistoric times when man crudely exploited iron and clay, and perhaps other metals, for the production of his cosmetics, crude implements and utensils. The early European explorers, mainly German, Spanish and British, located and mined tin, galena, gold, etc. for export to their home countries. Records show that organized exploration activities in Nigeria commenced in 1903 and 1904 when the Secretary of State for Colonies inaugurated mineral surveys of the Southern and Northern Protectorates respectively. The principal mineral occurrences discovered by the survey teams included lignite deposits at Asaba, lead-zinc ores at several locations in the south-east, monazite, limestone and lead-zinc ores at Abakaliki district. Others were coal at Enugu, brine springs at Arufu and Awe, Galena,tin and columbite in Jos area, iron ore deposits in Niger and Kwara districts and marble deposits in Jakura. Mining activity in controlled form, however, commenced in the country in 1915 with the production of coal at the Enugu mines.

Thought even went ahead to argue that the discoveries and sourcing of these minerals is the prime objective of colonialism. The minerals were probably discovered in the early twentieth century, approximately in 1892. Railway tracks were built throughout the country linking different regions that have raw materials to the main grid to help them collect these raw materials and transport them south to the sea port at Lagos for export. The collection system was done in such a way that important stations along the rail routes were constructed whereby the raw materials could be loaded into the train wagons. Tin has greatly aided the United Kingdom's war effort during the First World War in 1915-18 and even during the Second World War in 1939-1945. It supplements the great demand for other heavy minerals to boost the high industrial demand of raw materials to feed the royal industries and manufacture armaments for the famous global conflicts.

Nigeria is endowed with enormous mineral resources which when properly harnessed can lead to its industrial development and prospects. It is a known fact that countries abundantly endowed with mineral resources become great industrial nations (Okpanachi, 2004). While on the other hand, the level of greatness of a nation is often a reflection of how its resources have been planned, managed and utilized (Gotan, 2004). The occurrence of mineral resources in commercial quantities alone does not however guarantee optimum benefit, factors such as technological capacity, finance and market are also equally important.

Nigeria is endowed with numerous mineral resources which are at various stages of development. Most of the development however is done by informal and artisanal miners who lack the appropriate technology and funds to carry out the exploitation in a sustainable manner, as result they leave behind a devastated landscape which adversely affects the various environmental media and its resources like water, soil and food crops as well as the health of humans and animals.

Nigeria is blessed with Huge Tin Ore reserves. Nigeria's Jos Plateau, was once the hub of a mining industry which fed European demand for tin through much of the 20th century. Tin mining in Plateau began in October 1904 when the British colonial government sent a mineral-survey team to assess the mineral deposits within the region. Tin deposits were discovered in the Jos-Plateau area and foreign companies were allowed by the colonial regime to operate in the territory and mine the resources, using mechanized equipment which helped to curb the risks and prevent the death of the mine workers. Today, Nigeria is the second largest tin producing country in Africa, just above Russia globally, although it has the reserves to sustain a much larger production with more investment. Nigeria's reserves are located in Plateau, Kano, Ondo, Nassarawa, Kwara, Bauchi, and Osun states Nigeria's mineral resources and mining industry have witnessed several stages of development from the era of traditional mining during which there were no policies or legislation governing the industry (Pre-colonial era) to the era marked by proper documentation of all mining activities in the country, known as the colonial era (Davou and Dung Gwom, 2008). The post colonial era witnessed various government policies and programmes on the minerals sector as well as a high level of instability. This period coincided with the advent of petroleum, and brought about a drastic shift in labour and government attention from the solid mineral industry and agriculture to the petroleum industry, the result of which is a decline in the mineral industry up to 1980 and 1990s when the industry was at the verge of collapse. The Nigeria Government viewed the solid mineral industry as a profit oriented sector, and became involved in exploration, exploitation and marketing of solid minerals as observed by the setting up of the Nigeria Mining Corporation (NMC) in 1973. The Nigeria Mining Corporation could not achieve much as petroleum continued to dominate the mining industry and the National economy (Davou and Dung –Gwom, 2008).In an attempt to reverse the reliance on petroleum, a bold step was taken to revamp the solid mineral industry through the establishment of the then Ministry of Solid Mineral Development in 1995, which today is known as the Ministry of Mines and Steel development. This ministry is now restructured and a new law, the Nigeria minerals Mining act, 2007, and also a National minerals and metals policy (January 2008) put in place. Similarly several agencies (e.g. the Geological Survey agency and mining cadastre) under the Ministry have been restructured to ensure better performance in the sector. Despite all of this development, the industry is still far from achieving its goals.

1.2 PLATEAU THE BEAUTIFUL

The area which is today known as Plateau State was located in the north central region of the present day Nigeria. Some referred to it as the middle belt region. The region occupied a unique position on the map of Nigeria, almost located at the central part. The region has exquisite features which include high terrain with looming rocky outcrops, beautiful landscapes and extended mountain ranges like the shere hills and tall mountains peaks like the Wase rock, Dogon Dutse amongst others. The dominant mountain types in this region are dormant volcanoes. The characteristic hilly nature of this region had indicated the presence of underground minerals, given birth as a result of tectonic processes in the earth crust and the cool weather speeds up the solidification process.   So many solid minerals were discovered in this region, some of which are Quartz, Zircon, Feldspar, Topaz, Tommaline, Aquar marine, Fish eye, Tin, Columbite, and Tantalite etc. But the once found in large quantities are Tin and Columbite. Between the two, Tin is obviously the prominent and this is not unconnected to its early discovery. Imperial geologist discovered these minerals during the colonial era. The British colonialists have discovered several solid minerals and other raw materials in all their crown colonies.

In Nigeria, according to the tourism master plan developed in 1990, five major tourism clusters have been identified. These include the Sahara gateway, Scenic heartland, Capital conference centre, South east and Atlantic gateway clusters. Three of these five clusters, which include Scenic Heartland, Capital Conference and South East, are geotourism based. The Scenic heartland is almost entirely covering the Jos Plateau, the wisdom and concept of the developers essentially based on climatic, cultural and scenic beauties of the Plateau. Ogezi et al. (2010) highlighted that Plateau State has the most striking physical features in Nigeria with the highlands rising from 1,200 meters above sea level and the low lands to a peak of 1,829 meters above sea level. Some of these classical geotourism landmarks of the Plateau include Wase Trachyte-Phonolite Plug, Kurra and Assop Water Falls, Surra Volcanic Line, Luham Rock, Riyom Rock, Kwi Conical Hill and Kerang Volcanic Hill, Shere Hills, Pankshin Hilltop, The Pudong ("Pidong") Crater Lake, Gahwang and Yembe Fall Columnar Basalts. More than half of the tourist landmarks in Plateau state are geological in nature such that the acronym home of "peace and geotourism" for the state would still have been appropriate.

Aside from Wase rock, all the tourist landmarks are directly related to the uplift due to the emplacement of the Younger granites which form the core of the Jos Plateau. The Falls are also caused by the steep gradients generated by the uplift of the Plateau. The Kwi hills were possibly formed by lateralization of the Lower Cenozoic – Upper Cenozoic basalts in Nigeria (Woakes et al., 1989) while the Gahwang columnar basalts belong to the Younger flow volcanics of Nigeria.

Remains of Former Activity Madziarz (2013) documented that mining activity constitute a precious source of knowledge about the development of deposit mining technology, providing the evidence of knowledge and skills of the generations of miners connected over the centuries with the area of Lower Silesia. The treasures in mining do not only lie in the products themselves but also in the history that their extraction carries both during and after the mining. Mining on the Plateau at present has left traces of what at best can be referred to as historical artifacts of mining. All over the plateau, ponds and disturbances dot the landscape.

Plateau State (capital, Jos) is the twelfth largest state in Nigeria by area size, occupying a surface area of 26,899 square kilometers; it gets its name from the beautiful Jos Plateau. Located in Nigeria's middle belt, to its North, are Kaduna and Bauchi States while Benue State is at its Southern border. It is flanked in the east by Taraba State and in the west by Nassarawa State. The unique physical features of Plateau State (Home of Peace and Tourism) are its high relief; a combination of a mountainous area with captivating rock formations, punctuated by deep gorges, lakes, bare rocks, rivers, waterfalls that define its grass lands especially in the north, and its geological history. The high relief, or more appropriately, the Jos Plateau, provides a hydrological centre for many rivers in northern Nigeria and confers on the northern part of the state a cool climate suitable for livestock rearing and growing of exotic crops. The process of formation of its high relief makes Plateau State one of the States in the country with rich mineral resources. It has a temperate climate on the Jos Plateau and a hot and humid climate on its lower parts. Generally, weather conditions are warmer during the rainy season (April – October) and much colder during the harmattan period (December –

February). Harnessing the Resources of the Jos Plateau for Sustainable Development Plateau State boasts of abundant agricultural and mineral resources, the soil and climatic conditions of the Jos Plateau favor the production of exotic crops like Irish potatoes, apples, grapes, wheat, barley and vegetables. The region produces about 200,000 tons of Irish potatoes annually. These crops are grown throughout the year, irrigated during the dry season. The State has an estimated cattle population of 1.07 million in the hands of the Fulani nomads. A little less than half of these cattle, graze permanently on the cool tsetse-fly free Jos Plateau, while the remainder spend the dry season on the rangelands of Benue plains and move up to the Plateau in the wet season. Plateau State is endowed with rich deposits of a variety of industrial minerals of high quality.

Tin and columbite have been mined on the Jos Plateau since 1902. Although production has declined, due to a drastic fall in demand, this area was once the world's leading producer of tin with an annual output of 17,000 tons in the peak war period of 1941-45. Other minerals found in Plateau State in commercial quantities are barytes, kaolin, zircon, monazite, marble, limestone, sphalerite, quartz, galena, glass sand, clay and gemstones. Fish farming has gradually become a major economic activity in the State. A modern hatchery with a capacity to produce two million fingerlings of tilapia, carp and mudfish for sale to farmers has been established, as well as pond fisheries consultancy service unit to stimulate private investment in fish farming to boost the industry Plateau State is known as "The Home of Peace and Tourism" and there is plenty to see, ranging from the Wildlife Safari Park which is about 4 km (2 mi) from Jos, and offers a wide variety of wild animals: buffalos, lions, leopards, baboons, monkeys, derby elands, pythons, crocodiles, chimpanzees, jackals and the rare pygmy hippopotamus, which is being successfully bred in the 'hippo pool'. Other notable tourist destinations in the State are; The National Museum in Jos, The Museum of Traditional Nigerian Architecture, Assop Falls, Wase Rock, The Kerang highlands, The Shere Hills, Riyom Rock, Pandam Game Reserve, Kahwang Rock, etc.

It is general knowledge that the revenue profile of the "Tin City" will receive significant boost should the environment be made more conducive for private investors to harness the rich agricultural and mineral development potentials of the State. Even though many industries have started to take advantage of the abundant raw materials in the State, including Makeri Smelting Company, Kaolin industry in Barakin Ladi, Gold and Base, Exiands and Kaduna Prospectus and other agro-based types utilising local agricultural materials such as NASCO Foods, NASCO Packs, Jos International Breweries, Northern Nigeria Fibre Products and Grand Cereal and Oil Mills Limited.

1.3 GENERAL DESCRIPTION, IMPORTANCE AND USES OF TIN AND COLUMBITE:

An established and well managed Tin and Columbite solid mineral sub-sector will accelerate economic, social and political growth of Nigeria by provision of gainful employment and a rise in national income earnings far exceeding the petroleum sector. In addition, tin and columbite will provide local raw materials for industries and bring vital infrastructure and wealth to rural areas.

Tin and Columbite contributed immensely to the economic development of Nigeria in the pre-independence years. During this period, Nigeria was known for the production and exportation of Tin, Columbite, Lead and Zinc. Nigeria was the largest producer of Columbite at one point and the sixth world producer of Tin at another time. The earnings from Tin and columbite minerals were used to develop roads,

28

education, hospitals and in fact develop the petroleum industry.

The decline of the tin and Columbite minerals sub-sector of the solid minerals industry started with the discovery of oil to an extent that Nigeria became a mono product economy and vulnerable to international oil politics. The domineering role of oil did not allow past governments to attend to global challenges that evolved in the development of solid minerals.

The neglect of Tin and Columbite minerals industry led to disorder in the mines field with strong presence of illegal miners whose activities are characterized by inefficient mining, illegal trading of highly priced minerals, severe ecological degradation, spread of diseases and huge loss of revenue to the government through smuggling.

On the other hand, Mining continues to play a key role in the development of Africa's economies. Countries like South Africa, Ghana and Tanzania, remain critically dependent on the earnings of solid minerals. As a result, countries introduced liberal reforms to meet intense competition to attract investment funds. Ghana for example undertook significant reforms both in legal and institutional frame-work and to the general organization of the sector. The result has been growth in mining investment. Tanzania is now a leading destination for exploration funds due to the deliberate government attention to the development of mining. Burkina Faso and Mali have also become strong mining countries. Following the global economic recession of the late 1980s and early 1990s, developing countries started liberalizing their external trade to improve balance of payment, increase economic growth through the provision of incentives to attract capital in-flow and investment.

The developing countries especially in Africa and Latin America turned to Solid Minerals exploration as a solution to sustained economic growth. Nigeria's economy which is largely dependent on a mono-product (petroleum) became vulnerable to fluctuations in oil prices with the attendant shocks on the economy. This informed the Federal Government's decision to diversify the nation's economic base from oil to the non-oil sectors including the development of solid minerals resources. Some of such minerals that have been identified for development are tin and Columbite ores. Tin ore (Cassiterite) is the second –easiest ore to mine after Columbite ore (Niobium). Tin ore is mined from tin veins. Cassiterite is a tin oxide mineral, SnO_2. It is generally opaque but it is translucent in thin crystals. Its luster and multiple crystal faces produce a desirable gem. Cassiterite has been the chief tin ore throughout ancient history and remains the most important source of tin today.

Tin ore is employed in plating, production of tin oxide used in paint, paper and ink industries, production of tin oxide resistors and electric lead wires. Tin is used to produce tinplate, or steel coated with tin, which is used for food packaging. Tin and tin alloys are used also for solder, especially in the electronics industry. It is commonly used as an alloy for bearing metal and as an alloy in metallic coatings. The inorganic compounds of tin are used in ceramics and glazes. Organic compounds

31

of tin are used in plastics, wood preservatives, pesticides and in fire retardants. The tin mining ponds can be used for irrigation farming during the dry seasons. The ponds can be used for fishing (fish ponds). Mining ponds for instance, can be converted to resort, as in the case of Ray field resort for various recreational activities.

The second such minerals that have been identified for development is columbite ore. It is known to occur in Plateau and latter, Kano, Kaduna, Bauchi, Kogi, Kwara and Nasarawa States. Because of the numerous uses of Columbite, there is steady and increasing demand for the product. Columbite, also called niobite, niobite-tantalite and columbite [(Fe, Mn) Nb_2O_6], is a black mineral group that is an ore of niobium. It has a sub metallic luster and a high density and is a niobate of iron and manganese.

Columbite has the same composition and crystal symmetry (orthorombic) as tantalite. In fact, the two are often grouped together as a semi-singular mineral series called columbite-tantalite or coltan in many mineral guides. However, tantalite has a much greater specific gravity than columbite, more than 8.0 compared to columbite's 5.2.

Columbite is also very similar to tapiolite. Those minerals have same chemical composition but different crystal symmetry: orthorhombic for columbite and tetragonal for tapiolite. The largest documented single crystal of columbite consisted of plates 6 millimeters (0.24 in) thick measuring 76 by 61 centimeters (30 × 24 in).

Source of columbite ore used as an alloy of steel to form weldable high speed steel for radio transmitting valves, heat sensitive detective devices called barometer, for jet engines and other aircraft components. Coltan or Columbite Tantalite is used primarily for the production of tantalum capacitors, used in many electronic devices. It is also used in high temperature alloys for air and land based turbines. The upsurge in electronic products over the past decade resulted in a peak in late 2000 with inflated high demand and price increases for the mineral which lasted a few months.

CHAPTER 2:

2.0 THE TIN CITY:

2.1 Tin & Columbite mining on the Jos Plateau; A historical perspective

The solid minerals mining industry which is also the largest producer of Tin & columbite on Jos Plateau started in 1902. The mining of tin has been largely responsible for profound changes in the landscape and in the social economic structure.

Mineral exploitation in Plateau State is an age-old industry, starting from the pre-colonial extraction and marketing of tin from the upper Plateau to salt and lead-zinc in the lower Plateau that includes Awe, a former local government of Plateau State now part of Nassarawa State.

Officers of the Niger Royal Company were credited with locating tin deposits of Jos Plateau which had marked the inception of modern mining activities in Nigeria. Foreign metal merchants, mostly British, followed the tin trade route from the North African markets into Nigeria to Plateau where an aggressive and prosperous tin mining industry was established. Subsequently, the multinational companies, which dominated the industry, were joined by small local companies. While the foreign companies congregated under powerful chambers of mines, the local miners formed themselves under a less powerful organization called the "Association of African Miners."

The tin trade boomed to the detriment of other minerals in the state. There was then the dominance of Nigerian mining activities by British companies with the backing of British banking service and supplies. At the peak of mining, there were up to 120 companies operating. Then, mining was exclusively a private sector affair. During this time, it came to a point that Nigeria was the sixth world producer of tin with a production of 16 000 tons per annum and world's leading producer of columbite.

The Association of African Miners became heavily handicapped by a myriad of problems, ranging from lack of necessary expertise to a dearth of capital and hence the necessary equipment required for efficient performance in the field. With the aforementioned, the multinational companies piled up and repatriated huge profits while their African counterparts performed sluggishly, resorting sometimes to unorthodox practices but still managing to record success, which sometimes was questionable. The tin & Columbite mining industry was swept off the Nigerian economic scene by the so-called oil boom.

During this period the government concerned itself with providing the enabling environment and necessary infrastructure in the mines field and collected royalties, rents and related rates which before the mid-fifties were collected by the Niger Royal Company. Before the takeover of the collection, the Nigerian Government has to pay an all lump compensation to United African Company (UAC). Mining operations were effectively monitored by the mines division of the then Ministry of Mines and Power to ensure compliance with the operational and safety guidelines.

In 1972 the government indigenization decree led to the compulsory acquisition of controlling shares in the foreign companies. The foreigners then lost interest in mining operations. The activities of the companies declined slowly until they finally left the mining scene in the early eighties. This led to the merger of major companies to form what is today known as Consolidated Tin Mines (CTM). CTM could not work with the obsolete machineries left behind by the expatriates. The result now is a company struggling to survive. Also in 1972, the Nigerian Mining Corporation with headquarters in Jos was established to embark on exploitation of industrial minerals. The corporation discovered barytes at Azara in the present Nassarawa State and also established a barytes mine at the locality. This led to the discovery of the same mineral in Langtang South. Kaolin was also discovered at Kuba on the Barkin Ladi- Bokkos road and exploitation commenced in 1988.

2.2 Influx of workers

As the mining of Tin on the Plateau became extensive and popular, many migrant workers and their families from different parts of the country began to arrive in trickle at first and subsequently in their hundreds and then in the thousands in search of greener pastures. This is typical of most mining activities around the world where there are discoveries of precious minerals and you find massive population emigration and explosion.

Like the popular "Gold rush" of the 19th century in the Western fronts (Wild West) where there was mass exodus of people from Europe to the new land known today as the United States of America. Then, despite the challenges posed by unfamiliar new territories, coupled with aggressive tribal red skin Indians and harsh climatic conditions but yet they were willing to risk their life and that of their families for better life in a distant land because of the lure of precious minerals discoveries.

This can also be said of the discovery of Tin and columbite on the Plateau where large groups of people emigrated from different regions of Nigeria and beyond and settle in their new stations in groups and irrespective of the odds, are willing to change the course of their fortune in their new territory.

2.3 Category or classification of workers

With the influx of workers there also arise organizational structure and categorization at the mining sites. The first categories are the white expatriates or Directors, their African subordinates called them the 'Ogas'. The white miners themselves are answerable to the colonial crown. The white miners are the main supervisors on site because of their proficiency in the field. Sometimes, they double as client and supervisors at the same time exporting the proceeds directly abroad.

As the system was at that time, they perform both administrative and technical roles on site, even though they are being assisted by foremen.

The foremen at any mining site fall into the second category of mining workers. They receive direct orders from their white supervisors on what to do for the day and how to achieve targets by co-coordinating the affairs of workers directly under them. The foreman should be someone who have some knowledge of both Tin and Columbite minerals mining and should command the use of English language to be able to communicate with his white superiors. This he does by receiving directive from the white 'oga' and disseminates it very well to his subordinates in the general local language they understood.

Also, the foreman should be versatile enough to understand the dominant indigenous dialect spoken on site to be able to interact very well with his boss and the workers. The foremen themselves periodically engage in physical menial jobs while at the same time supervising the inputs of others.

The third categories of workers on the early mining sites are the assistants or otherwise known as the personal assistants (PA) to the white miners. For Tin and columbite mining activities on the Plateau, majority of the early personal assistants (about 80%) to the white miners are from southern Nigeria specifically the then mid-western region that is the urhobo speaking people. They probably attain these positions because of their good educational background and spoken English as a result of early contact with the whites who first came to Nigeria through the coastal regions.

Note here that among the remaining 20% that constitute the personal assistants of the white miners then are derived from the foremen who have long and distinguished service career with the white boss who latter absolve them as their assistants.

The assistants could read and write and therefore kept record of all workers on site under their payroll and take stock of materials because of their direct involvement with day to day activities on site. Sometimes, they are even assigned to pay workers remuneration. They are also assigned to recruit daily, weekly or monthly laborers because of their close contact and interaction with them. They knew most or almost all the workers personally by names, strength and temperament.

The position of any foreman during the early mining period is second only to the white boss. Generally, their role can be summarized as second degree supervision and first degree assisting. Combining these crucial roles together required a person of strong character.

The fourth categories of mining workers are the Technicians. They are strictly skilled set of workers who handles the equipments and machineries of operation such as trolleys, vertical lift, conveyors, Rigs, tracks and many other tools and machines. The white expatriates trained a substantial number of local miners to work as technicians alongside their mining engineers. The operators are specialized labor force in the mining sites and they enjoy better wages and welfare only second to the personal assistants. In some mining companies, living quarters are provided to them so as to be near the site for easy access in case of machine or equipment failure.

The fifth classification of mining site workers are the Laborers. These are further sub-divided into surface and underground laborers. The surface laborer, like their underground counterparts does the main tedious jobs. They gathered the 'telling' (unprocessed ore) through water way channels and through surface excavation not more than 3m deep.

On the other hand, the underground laborers do the mighty and dangerous work amongst all the aforementioned category of mining site workers. The nature of their work qualify them for some special bonuses especially if they 'hit the core', meaning if they find the main tin ore and excavate it. The digging is so tedious because they mostly used crude implements underground like diggers, shovels, heavy harmers and so on. The underground tunnels could be as long as half a kilometer in some places. The pits avoid hard underground rock outcrops by meandering around them in a changed direction. Principally, the direction of underground pit movement is determined by the available line of tin ore found.

The diggers worked day and night shifts and only come out of the 'Loto'(underground tunnel) only when their shifts is over. The underground passage ways or tunnels could have a width of up to 3meters in some areas to allow for the movement of excavated ore stacked in mini trolleys to designated collection points to the surface. The diggers used forehead lamps powered by oil for both day and night shifts as the pits are mainly dark.

In the cause of operation, sometimes weakness or fault lines may occur. Example, weak strata or large cracks which can jeopardize the operation on the tunnel ceiling or walls. Most at times these volatile regions are observed to have large content of very rich tin and columbite minerals ore. The temptation of the presence of these high grade minerals will override the needful to abandon the area and mark it as a danger zone. The white engineers and their technicians will be call upon and lowered into the tunnel to carry out repairs and maintenance. The Technical crew may use hard timber or steel as props to shore the ceiling up to prevent excessive weight leading to collapse. For the weak walls, the technicians will use iron bar struts to brace and strengthen the walls.

The last category of mining site workers are shed workers. This set of workers perform their function on the surface and mostly under provided canopies or shed to process the mineral ores(This formed the name of "tin shed" as popularly used everywhere in the mining industry then and today) being dug underground. They are involved in so many surface activities themselves but not as tedious and dangerous as those underground. Some of their work includes washing, drying, sieving, and jigging, machine operation, weighing and bagging.

2.4 Development of the Town

The first Nok terracotta was discovered in 1928 by Colonel Dent Young, a co-owner of a mining partnership, near the village of Nok on the Jos Plateau in Nigeria. The terracotta was accidentally unearthed at a level of 24 feet from an alluvial tin mine. Young presented the sculptures to the museum of the Department of Mines in Jos.

Fifteen years later, in 1943 near the village of Nok, in the center of Nigeria, a new series of clay figurines were discovered by accident while mining tin. A clerk in charge of the mine had found a head and had taken it back to his home for use as a scarecrow, a role that it filled (successfully) for a year in a yam field. This scarecrow was eventually noticed by Bernard Fagg who at the time was an administrative officer who had studied archaeology at the University of Cambridge. Fagg noticed that the head on the scarecrow looked similar to the sculpture that Young had found. He traveled to Jos where Young showed Fagg other recently uncovered terracotta figures. Eventually it became clear that the tin mining in Nok and Jema'a areas were revealing and destroying archaeological material.

Ames, a British colonial administrator, said that the original name for Jos was Gwosh which was a village situated at the current site of the city; according to Ames, the Hausa wrongly pronounced Gwosh as Jos and it stuck. According to the historian Sen Luka Gwom Zangabadt, the area known as Jos today was inhabited by indigenous ethnic groups who were mostly farmers. According to Billy J. Dudley, the British colonialists used direct rule for the indigenous ethnic groups on the Jos plateau since they were not under the Fulani emirates where indirect rule was used.

According to the historian Samuel N Nwabara, the Fulani empire controlled most of northern Nigeria, except the Plateau province. It was the discovery of tin by the British that led to the influx of other ethnic groups such as the Urhobos,Yoruba,Hausa, Igbo, and the Europeans ,thus making Jos a cosmopolitan city.

The Jos Plateau is a plateau located near the centre of Nigeria. It covers 8600 km² and is bounded by 300-600 meter escarpments around much of its circumference. With an average altitude of 1280 metres it is the largest area over 1000 metres in Nigeria, with a high point of 1829 metres in the Shere Hills. The plateau has given its name to the State, Plateau State in which it is found and is itself named for the state's capital, Jos.

The Jos Plateau is dominated by three rock types. The Older Granites date to the late Cambrian and Orduvician. The Younger Granites are emplacements dating to the Jurassic,and forming part of a series that includes the Aïr Massif in the central Sahara. There are also many volcanoes and sheets of basalt extruded since the Pliocene (Morgan 1983).

The Younger Granites contain tin which was mined since the beginning of the 20th century, during and after the colonial period.

The climate on the Plateau is the semi-temperate climate with temperatures ranging from 18 °C (64.4 °F) to 25 °C (77.0 °F).

The Jos Plateau is home to the ancient Nok culture, known for its remarkable terracotta artwork.
After the British colonization of Nigeria, Jos Plateau

became a mining region and one of the most important tourist destinations in Nigeria,

The Jos Plateau lies in the Nigerian Middle Belt, and even in this region known for cultural diversity, it is unusually diverse. Barbour et al. (1982:49) show over 60 ethno-linguistic groups on the plateau. Most of the plateau's languages are in the Chadic family (Isichei 1982), which is part of the Afro-Asiatic family.

The plateau is home to West Africa's only population of klipspringer (*Oreotragus oreotragus*), as well as several endemic birds and mammals, including Nigerian mole-rat (*Cryptomys foxi*) and Fox's shaggy rat (*Dasymys foxi*) the rock firefinch (*Lagonosticta sanguinodorsalis*) and the Jos Plateau indigobird (*Vidua maryae*).[2]

Situated almost at the geographical centre of Nigeria and about 179 kilometres (111 miles) from Abuja, the nation's capital, Jos is linked by road, rail and air to the rest of the country. At an altitude of 1,217 m (3,993 ft) above sea level, Jos enjoys a more temperate climate than much of the rest of Nigeria. Average monthly temperatures range from 21–25 °C (70–77 °F), and from mid-November to late January, night-time temperatures drop as low as 11 °C (52 °F). Hail sometimes falls during the rainy season because of the cooler temperatures at high altitudes. These cooler temperatures have meant that, from colonial times until the present day, Jos is a favorite holiday location for both tourists and expatriates based in Nigeria. Jos receives about 1,400 millimeters (55 inches) of rainfall annually, the precipitation arising from both convectional and orographic sources, owing to the location of the city on the Jos Plateau. According to the Köppen Climate Classification system, Jos has a Tropical savanna climate, abbreviated "Aw".

Jos is a great base for exploring the beauty of Plateau State. The Shere Hills, seen to the east of Jos, offer a prime view of the city below. Assop Falls is a small waterfall which makes a pleasant picnic spot on a drive from Jos to Abuja. Riyom Rock is a dramatic and photogenic pile of rocks balanced precariously on top of one another, with one resembling a clown's hat, observable from the main Jos-Akwanga road.

Tin mining has been one of the reasons behind the rapid

urban growth and expansion of Jos City. According to History tin mining started in Jos in1902 and by 1903, it was already discovered in Bukuru and later spread to Ropp and Barkin Ladi. Britain formally entered into tin ore exploration and mining in Plateau State during the industrial revolution in Europe, which made tin ore the number one foreign export from Nigeria, hence, large companies were also involved in the tin mining business and some individual had the opportunity to obtain license to mine on small scale. In 1760 to 1770, there were 13 indigenous blacksmith smelters in Naraguta village in Jos North local council. Moreover, during that period, the indigenous ethnic groups were discovering and producing tin along River Dilimi near Jos. Countries like Spain and others imported tin for making gun barrels. During the World War1, there was a high demand for tin, since it was mostly used for ammunition and at the same time serves as source of revenue for the country.

It grew rapidly after the British discovered vast tin deposits in the vicinity. Both tin and columbite were extensively mined in the area up until the 1960s. They were transported by railway to both Port Harcourt and Lagos on the coast, and then exported from those ports. Jos is still often referred to as "Tin City". In 1967 it was made capital of Benue-Plateau State, becoming the capital of the new Plateau State in 1975.

Jos has become an important national administrative, commercial, and tourist centre. Tin mining has led to the influx of migrants, mostly Urhobos,Yorubas,Hausas,Igbos, and Europeans, who constitute a substantial population of Jos. This "melting pot" of race, ethnicity and religion makes Jos one of the most cosmopolitan cities in Nigeria. For this reason, Plateau State is known in Nigeria as the "home of peace and tourism".

CHAPTER 3:

3.0 TYPICAL MINING SITES, CLAIMS AND DUMPS:

Some mining sites are as large as five hectares of land or more. Some important strategic mining sites are located at Jos, Kwanga, Du, Kuru, Foron, Riyom, Mararaban Jama'a, Sabon Gida,(Bisichi), Barkin Ladi, Mista Ali. At the peak of mining in Jos Plateau, a typical mining site has close to four hundred miners working concurrently in any given time.

The typical layout of a standard mining site is comprised of three major zones. These are the excavation zone, the Storage zone, the processing zone (or Tin shed) and the dumping zone.

3.1 The excavation zone consists of surface channels and underground tunnels. The surface channels are further subdivided into Stream sources and Shallow Pits not beyond nine (9) feet. The underground tunnels are also subdivided into three subdivisions; these are deep vertical tunnels, deep horizontal tunnels and deep meandering tunnels.

3.2 The Storage zone is a type of warehouse constructed some distance away from the excavation zone and more closer to the processing zone. The reason for storage is to safe keep the ores against weather elements like rainfall and against theft. The already excavated ores must be processed while dry. The ores are normally bagged in sacks and well arranged in vertical piles kept in the warehouse and properly arranged to demarcate gap for ownership. Each miner distinguishes his property from others by using ink markers or Ball pens. Sometimes the Storage or warehouse is filled up to capacity to the extent that some of the bagged ores will be kept outside. When outside, especially during the rainy season, miners uses large polythene to cover the bagged ores and prevent rain from soaking them. This is because at the peak of tin and columbite mining activities on the Jos Plateau, there are so many numbers of miners queuing and waiting for their allocated time to process or dress their ores.

3.3 The Processing zone which is the third in this category mostly takes place in the Tin shed. The Tin shed is where the processing machines and equipments are situated. Most of the machines work on electrical power from the national grid or standby generators. Here, the Tin and Columbite ores are brought out from the Warehouse where they are stored and taken into the tin shed for processing.   There is also another small Store building attached to the main building or Store room which is adjoining the office occupied by the Chief operator or manager's office where working tools, maintenance equipments, stationeries, Testing facilities, spare parts, processed or finished products bought by the company are kept. This store is mostly controlled by the manager or chief operator and the key to this very important room or building is maintained by them.

All the company vehicles used in transporting the heavy tin and columbite ores from the excavation site to the warehouse, sometimes from the Store or warehouse to the tin shed and finally from the tin shed to the selling or export points are located at the parking lot of the tin shed. The types of vehicles used in transporting both unrefined ores and final products in those days are very strong vehicles which are mostly four (4) wheel drives and have auxiliary gears such as Land Rovers and Nissan Patrols. Some Tin Sheds have Restaurants and Rest room serving as resting and sleeping place for workers off their shifts.

3.4 The Dumping zone is an area preserved for the evacuation of waste materials of processing not valuable at that material point in time in the value chain. Most of the waste materials come from inside the tin shed from machine operation or outside the tin shed from ore (telling) washing, Boxing machine (Wilbi) and from Jigging. The dumping zone could be located within the tin shed compound or far away from it some tens of Kilometers from the tin shed.

In some sites where the overbearing stratum is very hard, large surface Crane excavators are deployed and the excavated ores are transported through long lines of conveyor belts to the processing section at the end of the conveyor. The processing section of the very large and heavy duty machine contains the crusher, filter, blower and separator. These types of machines are very expensive and are not common in most tin and columbite sites. The expatriates mainly use this type of equipment in very large mining sites having large quantities of mineral deposits and having very hard under layer.

3.5 MINING CLAIMS referred to the exclusive right of individuals, groups or companies to exploit certain defined and reserved site locations for the purpose of mining the area. Normally these areas are believed to contain large deposits of tin and columbite ores from geological survey carried long ago by the British geologists. Every mapped claim is indicated by beacons or profiles and tagged for easy recognition due to so many of them at different locations. Most mining claims owned by white miners which are not yet mined were transferred to their confidant assistants prior to leaving Nigeria.

3.6 MINING DUMPS are found around productive mining sites especially close distance away from tin sheds. While some could be located some kilometers away from the tin shed or processing zone where it is transported to the dump and continuously accumulated for long period of time. The dumping lands are obviously owned by the individuals or companies that are dumping waste on it. The dumped materials are mostly iron, zircon, monoxide, sand admixture etc. The dumps are of two types, those poured or dumped on the surface and those poured into already dug pits underground. Either way, they are left abandoned for a long period of time.

CHAPTER 4:

4.0 STRUCTURE OF A TYPICAL MINING COMPANY:

The federal ministry of solid minerals through the old Nigeria mining corporation is powered by legislation to regulate the activities of solid minerals in the country.

The state ministry of mines and industry act as the chief supervisory and regulatory body within Plateau state. Being in the exclusive list, The Federal government registers and issue licenses to mining individuals, partners and companies to establish their own companies. The fact remains, that the bulk of tin and columbite mining companies on the Plateau are mostly operated by private individuals or group of companies. I will concentrate on the structure of the mining industry under the tin and columbite solid mineral subsector under private individuals.

There are so many private owners (or directors as they are called) in and around Plateau state who manage their own affairs, most of these directors built their tin shed close to their private residence or as part of their residence, while others rent some kind of buildings and form their tin shed there. The directors' relationship with miners affects a lot of customers to their company.

The structure of a typical tin, columbite and tantalite mining company can best be represented in a graphical form. This can best be appreciated by a tree like relationship in an organogram.

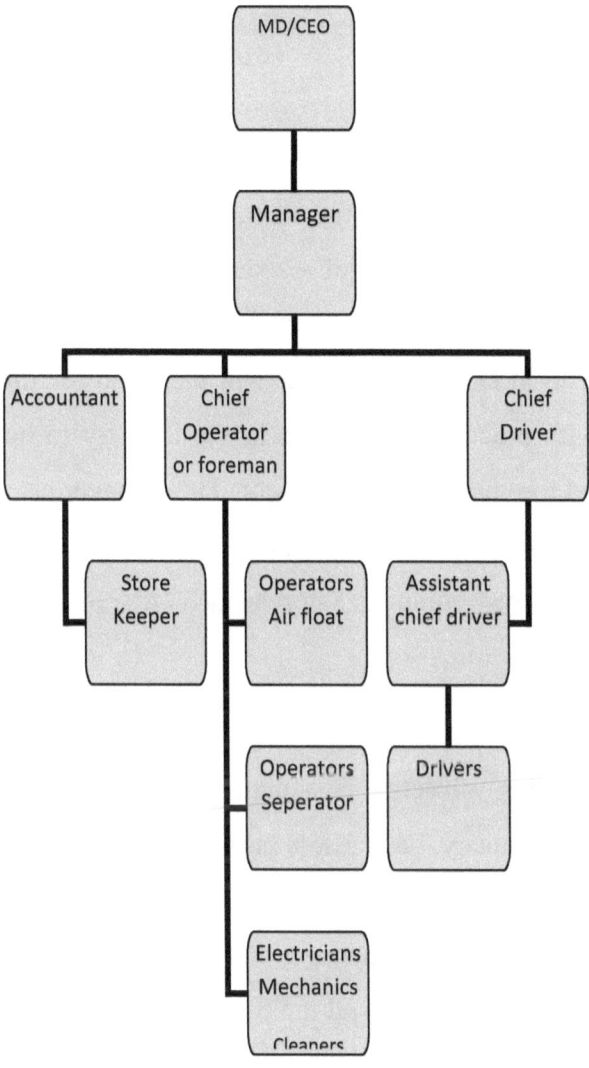

The company structure presented above is always headquartered in the processing zone particularly the tin shed.

4.1 Hierarchy

The hierarchy follows that the director which in most case is the owner and chief executive/M.D chooses someone who is experienced in the field to be his manager. The M.D or the manager will then also recruit someone with practical knowledge in the industry to be the Tin shed foreman or chief operator. The manager also employs air floaters, operators and others. The M.D or manager employs company storekeeper, drivers and office cleaners.

4.2 Roles

(i)**The managing director** is actually in the helm of affairs of the company, he is a sole proprietor who also is the main profiteer in any major deal. The MD employs his second in command or manager and pay him monthly wages the same way he pays all the company staffs under him. He has the power to hire or fire any category of worker in the company. The M.D's main responsibility is to negotiate business deals with contractors or foreign buyers interested in the product or if he can, to export the product abroad usually his presence in the company is not regular.

(ii)**The company manager** is the next in command to the M.D. He is respected and in most cases feared by his subordinates. He has the power to fire any company worker under him. A good manager that has sound public relation with customers can bring about success to the company, because he is in direct contact with staffs and customer every day, a manager's presence in the company should be regular and he must be able to carry everybody along. Most times, the manager and chief operator goes to sell the company's product without necessarily the M.D's presence there (even though he is aware).

Perhaps, due to the strategic position of a manager in a mining company, a company can succeed or fail. In other words, the success or failure of any mining company is directly proportional to the input of its manager. A mining company manager must be agile, industrious, and flexible and acts like an eagle at all times.

On several occasion, most companies crumble when a good manager stops working there or establish his own mining company. It was observed that most of the parent company customers follow him to become his customers and do business with him because of his antecedents, good P.R and good habit.

(iii)**The company Accountant** is mostly employed by the M.D and the person may not necessarily be experienced in the mining field. Possessing accounting skill was always the bases and criteria for employment. The accountant made account of business transactions carried out at the end of every business day. The accountant also kept and maintains record of all materials being bought by the company. The accountant also prepares payment vouchers and pays staff members their salary net at the end of every month with the exclusion of the manager (the manager is paid through cheque by the MD himself). The company manager sometimes verifies and even pays company staffs himself. The company accountant also maintains record of all existing and acquired stock in possession of the company like processing machines and equipments, machine spare parts, electrical lighting fittings and fixtures, sanitary and office stationeries. The accountant also issue out cash payments on a daily bases to customers who sold their products on the presentation of a slip of paper identifying the material type, quantity and grade which must be duly signed by the chief operator or foreman and counter signed by the manager of the company. Most mining company's accountants' doubles as their cashiers also, they lodge and withdrew money from the banks whenever needed.

The M.D directs the manager via the accountant to deduct a certain amount of money from the company's account for the purchase of materials for every business day. The M.D frequently conducts a thorough inspection of the company's accounts without prejudice to the manager or accountant. The M.D also kept separate account record for his own purpose.

(iv) **Foreman or chief operator's** duty is to ensure that all other operators are attending to customers and also all machines are operational. The chief operator is answerable to the company manager while all other operators are subordinates to him. Being highly technical, another very important function of the company fore man or chief operator is the buying of materials from customers. The chief operator or foreman has a table in a small adjoining office to the wide-open tin shed and in some places his table is situated at a corner of the tin shed itself. The office is a general purpose office where all the testing and measuring apparatus and equipments are kept. This office is unarguably the most visited office in the organization per day. The Chief operator or foreman is responsible for all necessary tests being conducted on mineral ores to ascertain their value before purchase. The foreman or chief operator equally weighs the processed material before writing the data on a piece paper which contains the value of the finished product like the grade, the weight and the name of the customer. With that in place, all the customer needs to do is to go and present the piece of paper to the accountant or cashier for payment. The foreman's function is that of absolute skill and knowledge in the areas of machinery handling, processing, testing, recording of any type of material than even managers and M.Ds could discern or do. Anything less, the company will be in for a lost. An inexperienced foreman or chief operator can buy garbage to the company which will eventually result to sell at a loss or re- processed at a high cost. Foremen or chief operators need to operate like "wizards" for recognizing, discerning and distinguishing good or bad materials.

In some small mining establishments, the managers test and buy materials for the company, which in itself is very tedious.

(v)**The operators** function is to operate the machines and help customers to dress or process their materials. They air-float materials and set any of the machines for those customers that did not know how to. In some mining tin sheds, no customer is allowed to touch any machine except the operators by order from the manager or M.D.

Some operators can carry out minor service of any faulty parts of the machine whenever the need arose.

Operators also dress the company's materials which are bought from customers whenever necessary. Most operators are former tin shed boys that have a lot of experience in the field. A regular tin shed boy with years of experience can carry out other activities mentioned previously including operating all the machines, that is why some operators are employed from amongst them.

(vi)**The company drivers** could be employed by the M.D or manager. A typical mining company will have about two or more land Rover vehicles. The Land Rover is the choice vehicle for miners and it gained popularity in the seventies, eighties and early nineties. Widely favored by miners because of its strength, durability and consistency with Nigeria roads especially hilly and rocky terrains, bush tracks and mud pot holes. Company driver's role are relevant than meet the eye. This is because majority of customers bringing fresh tailing material comes from and reside in the hinterlands or rural areas. The company in its bid to acquire more customers and large constant supply of fresh good grade mineral ores and unprocessed tailings, most companies will give the rural and some urban miners' loan and will subsidize their activities by providing free transportation from their villages with their tailing to the tin shed in the city to dress their materials. Sometimes the company issues out free meal tickets to their regular customers and goes to an extra mile of transporting them back freely especially when they are many and the quantity and quality of product sold is appreciable. This is one of the company strategies to maintain customers and keep their business running because without the customers, the company cannot thrive.

Therefore drivers, play a significant role in the company's business, they also transport the company's finished product or processed minerals to be sold. Company drivers also carry out other miscellaneous activities and errands like transporting the accountant to and fro banks regularly as dictated by the hierarchy.

CHAPTER 5:

5.0 CHARACTERISTICS OF THE INDUSTRY

There are so many characteristics associated with the tin and Columbite solid minerals mining sub sector which we cannot exhaust all of them, but amongst the most salient of them are:-

5.1 Fluctuation of prices; The frequent rise and fall of prices in the local and global market may be attributed to so many factors, some of which are high tariffs on exports and imports, discovery of better alternative minerals, and other economic indices driven by market forces as is the order in any free market economy.

In the local scene, sometimes rise in prices may be caused by some greedy directors who want to maximize their profit at the detriment of others. For example a director will rise up in a day and announce to his customers about a slight drop in the price of tin or columbite since most of the customers are under loan from the company, and are restrained from going to other companies for trial, their only alternative is to submit. He created the scenario referred to in some mining circles as "local deflation".

In this way the director will buy at a very low price from his customers and sell at regular price thereby maximizing profit at the expense of the peasant miners who have no way of verifying the true market price.

5.2 Global Market Influence; in the foreign market however, certain determinants dictate the fluctuation in price which simultaneously affect prices in the local market. Some of these determinants could be as a result of the discovery of similar mineral in other countries which sells at lower prices – this will force the prices in the global market to go bearish or downward.

The price of the same minerals could also rise up if some other countries discovered or revolutionize an important area of utilization of the mineral in their industrial technological sector to boost their economy. In the same vain the world market price of the minerals may also fall down if better alternative minerals were discovered and were scientifically and technologically tested to be more efficient and better replacement for the former minerals.

Another inseparable characteristic of the tin and columbite mining is

5.3 Fraudulent or sharp practices. This

misdemeanor error exist in all level of the hierarchy from some of the M.Ds themselves to the tin shed boys.

Some M.Ds nailed their contractors, while some managers and accountants engage in false accounting. Some chief operators or foreman connive to buy rubbish material or low grade materials as high grade materials to the company. Some tin shed boys steal from customer's material. Some air float operators' punch unseen holes on the top clothe of the air floating machine which allows much quantity of materials to fall down into the interior which they will latter in the absence of people loosen the machine and scoop it. The customers themselves are not left behind in their share of conducting sharp practices in the tin shed like selling only part of the processed minerals while secretly taking some minerals away to other places to sell at exorbitant prices.

Additives or popularly known as concoction in the mining circle is one of the worst aspect of the fraud we are talking about here. There was a time in the past that the local price of tin and columbite fell very low because a major exporter was humiliated abroad when the product he exported could not be bought because of the high presence of impurities.

What miners do in concoction was to mix two or different material products together, some heavier than the others so that the heavier one can boost the weight of the other and therefore increase its grade. So many examples abound viz

Example 1:

A processed columbite that reads 19.2 and 30 lbs (or pounds weight) will be mixed with a heavy monoxide of about 5 lbs. The material mixture could weigh about 35 lbs and the grade will shoot up to 18.9. When interpreted, that means more money per pounds of the mixture with better grades and larger quantity. Now the side effect is that the initially pure columbite which is dark blue in color will now have reddish particles in it. It is left for the buyer to use his discretion.

Example 2:

Tin is also used by dubious, miners to raise or increase weight of columbite which transcends to increasing the grade. 4 lbs of tin when thoroughly mixed with say 20 lbs of columbite will shoot up the columbites's grade with almost 3-4 points and increase the quantity. Even when the mixture is tested by burning, only an insignificant percentage will be seen

Example 3:

Wolfrormite which is a relatively heavy mineral is widely used in concoction or blending materials. Wolfromites are 16-17 grade materials, when substantial quantity is mixed with low grade columbite it can turn the columbite to high grade. It is not easily discernable because it looks like the columbite itself only when wolf test is carried out will it be identified by some buyers.

Another technique used by dubious miners is the adjustment of their scale balance. The balance is reduced to 2, 3, 4 or more points, so that after buretting your material will be 2, 3, 4 or more points lower than its actual grade. If the same material is to be taken to other scales somewhere else, it will be discovered that it is higher by the same number of points reduce at the previous place. This is common among the individual retail buyers.

Example: the actual grade of Mr. X columbite or tin is 20.0 but after taken it to Mr. Z's place to sell, the buretted result gives 20.5. Mr. X suspected the scale and disagrees out rightly with the result and then takes his columbite to a tin shed in town. After buretting, the results gives 20.0, He then decides to sell his material product at the company.

If Mr.X had sold his material product to Mr. Z earlier on, he would have incurred a loss of about 20% due to the difference of 5 points.

❖　　　　Another fraudulent way of making profit by miners is to reduce their weighing scale by 1 or 2 points. This is a direct way of cheating because the customers materials quantity will drop by 1 to 2 pounds and then the cheat will latter only have to convert the 1 or 2 pounds into monetary value. Some company's scale is one (1) pound short whether by omission or commission. This practice is more prevalent among the home retail buyers and the chief operators or foreman that buys material for the company.

❖　　　　Another crook method adopted by fraud miners is through the addition of additives. This special treatment is carried out so that the additive will not be detected. For example, a heavy monoxide will be burnt while mixed with kerosene or petroleum. After burning, the yellowish and reddish particles of the monoxide are burnt to black color still retaining its weight. Burnt monoxide will hardly be detected when mixed thoroughly with comparatively lager quantity of columbite.

The resulting effect is that this roasted monoxide will add more weight to the columbite and shoot its grade high even converting low grade into high grade.

❖ Lastly in this aspect, miners indulge in stealing their colleagues' materials, you dare not keep any good columbite or Tin in sight and leave the scene for some minutes, it will virtually disappear. That is why in some large mining companies we have day time security personnel employed monitor on activities so as to curtail such vices.

Tin shed boys, followed by operators are suspected to be the most active in this area. Once there is a case of theft in the tin shed, the principal suspects are the two categories mentioned above.

Operators, particularly air floaters device fraudulent means of exploiting customers. They do this by creating tiny holes in the yard covering the top of the Air float machine. This is so that during floating, columbite and tin will fall down as a result of gravity into the inner space of the air float machine. When the tin shed is less busy they will loosen the top platform or deck of the air float machine, all in the name of repairing the air float but they will evacuate the materials that fall inside.

5.4 Behavioral trends; this is an important but yet neglected characteristic of the tin and columbite mining industry. The behavioral characteristics refer to the attitude of the miners themselves towards their endeavor. The attitude of most miners towards their profession is mostly lukewarm and lackadaisical. A typical miner always seek for avenue to maximize profit by all means whether by good or by crook rather than looking at the professional aspect of the trade, they prefer to indulge in the financial side of it.

Average miners only rely on the short term rather than the medium term or long term benefits. They so much dwell on the present as against the future. Most miners do not see mining of tin and columbite and other minerals as a profession that should be treated with uttermost regard they only view it as a means to an end. This probably justify why the zeal to further expand on their knowledge and skill of tin and columbite mining is truncated, this in itself is a mega problem which when unchecked will lead to a downward trend in the mining industry.

CHAPTER 6:

6.0 VISIBLE EVIDENCE OF NEGLECT AND DETERIORATION IN THE INDUSTRY

The physical evidence of neglect and abandonment is all around us. The almost deserted mines where extraction takes place use to accommodate hundreds of prospective miners. On the other hand, machines used in the past can be seen scattered about the expanse of the zone and left rusting in the weather.

6.1 Abandoned Mine Sites; the area that suffers much neglect is the extraction stage which is the primary source of the raw ore. The extraction of the mineral ore had largely suffered neglect ever since the departure of white miners after independence. The little or absence of geological skill by indigenous geologists may have been one of the reasons for the backwardness in discovering more potential sites. The result is that the sites being discovered long ago by the white mining geologists are outsourced and exhausted to the point of collapse. Plateau State is believed to have very large deposit reserve of tin and columbite which are still untapped. This is evident by the amount of materials still being excavated and brought to the city for processing. The problem is that some minerals are only found deep down (some up to 30m deep in the earth crust) and it will take modern underground equipments and machines to mine them. With the present order of things at the present generation of mining a lot need to be done.

6.2 Machine rust; a lot of excavation equipments at the present are obsolete to suit modern mining requirements. Many local miners can undergo the rigorous labor with simple tools to excavate ore deep in the earth, but little or no patronage or sponsorship hinders their effort. All these culminate into abandoned mine sites, machine and equipment rusting and the deterioration of the industry as a whole. Many machines at the extraction and production levels remains and continue to remain idle because of insufficient raw material (mineral ore) availability with more raw material ore, tin sheds will became fully alive and busy and cash circulating in the system.

6.3 Unemployment; Tin and columbite mining on the Plateau have been the bedrock of the State's economy for a very long time and the major source of income and means of employment for millions of people within and outside it since inception. It provides means of career and provisional employment to many in the section of extraction and excavation, production, transportation and exportation.

Tin and columbite mining does not need any pre-qualification for starters. A novice to the field only need to be cautious and attach himself to those that are familiar with the business for a while afterward the newcomer can decide which aspect of mining he want to join – buying and selling, as a company staff or a laborer depending on his orientation.

Due to the downward trend of tin and columbite mining on the Plateau, a lot of people particularly the youth (about 87% youths dominated) became unemployed and had look elsewhere for their sustenance . Unemployment as result of the neglect and deterioration of the industry has left many people both young and old, educated and non-educated roam about in search of income source replacement which obviously was difficult to come by.

I remembered when the industry was booming; whenever you go to any tin shed you will think it is a mini market place.   A lot of people join mining business because of its lucrative business nature with relatively high profit making and instant cash payment. One can mobilize any material, buy it, wash it, dress it and make eye watering profit which can replicate your startup capital geometrically by 7 to 10 times more than the initial capital all in the space of one (1) to two (2) days. Tin and columbite mining which unarguably is the biggest employer of labor in the tin city in the past years has now become shadow of its old self.

CHAPTER 7:

7.0 REASONS FOR NEGLECT

Possible causes of Neglect but not limited to the following

7.1 Lack of government interest:

Mining both (liquid & solid) belongs to the exclusive list. This explains why government was deeply involved in the mining of solid minerals and in particular tin &columbite on the Plateau since the turn of the twentieth century.

Prior to Nigeria's independence, the first oil was discovered in Oloibiri in 1953. Through the sixties, oil mineral was mined in large quantity from the southern delta confluence region. Subsequently, Nigeria government interest began to drift away from the previous sources of its income (which includes groundnut, cotton, cocoa tin, columbite to mention but a few) to crude oil the precious liquid gold as is referred to in some quarters.

The oil boom of the 70's further took the government interest a distance away from the other source of its income. The country become rich and is basking in Affluence from the proceed of crude oil sells. There was high demand for crude oil around the world at that period to power the industrial might of the super powers competing with each other and the other advance countries of Europe and Asia (Japan then).

Government become oblivious of the other sectors from the mid 70's to the present time and focused more on crude oil revenue and this lead to the neglect and downward fortune of other sectors of the economy that are meant to generate revenue.

7.2 Poor management practices:

The Europeans are the sole managers of the mining of tin and columbite on the plateau. Being naturally good in management and maintenance, they handle the mining industry very well for decades.

They carry out regular maintenance of machines, import new and improved machines. They conduct the day to day activities in the industry very well through on site constant supervision and direct employment of workers.

Through the years, the Europeans pass on their mining skills to their close confidants or their secretaries and assistants who are more educated than the laborers and foremen. Most of the secretaries came from the Urugbo tribe of the southern part of Nigeria. At that period of leaving back to their countries the white handed over all their properties, holdings and stakes to their close confidants and assistants as mentioned earlier.

The late 70's and early 80's saw the Urogbos owning most of the big mining companies in Jos. Some of which are C.A MENTA, at Apata, MONONIA, Ogboloco Nig Ltd etc.

Mining of tin and columbite thrived well for sometime in plateau state after the exit of the Europeans because they have passed on their knowledge to the indigenous people. After sometime, the management of the companies become challenging and difficult particularly in the early nineties when most of the first generation miners who got training from the white miners became very old and retired from active participation. They are seldom seen in tin sheds or any mining sites. They passed the routine administration of the mining companies to their direct descendants who have staggered knowledge of the technical, administrative and managerial skills required for a successful business as exhibited by the Europeans and their assistants after them. Some other salient reasons may be attributed to the following viz;-

- Non maintenance culture of Nigerians
- obsolete machinery and none update of same
- Many children and wives which eat deep into the capital of the companies.
- Amongst others

By the time the direct beneficiaries of the companies from Europe become very old to manage the mining companies they pass the leadership to their children who have limited knowledge of mining as oppose to their parents.

Sometimes it was tussle for leadership control of the companies between half siblings that result to further aggravate the industry's problems. The vacuum created by the exit of the Europeans from tin and columbite mining on the Plateau could not be filled by Nigerians despite the training they received from them.

7.3 Absence of regulator(s) direct involvement

The genuine regulator of mining activity in Nigeria is the former ministry of mines and power now under the Federal ministry of solid minerals.

For tin and columbite mining on the Plateau, the regulators are both the Plateau State government and the Federal government of Nigeria. These regulators are mostly absent at the various stages of production. At any point in time you could hardly find any regulator's supervisors on any mining site at the excavation point in the rural area to the processing & exporting point in the urban areas.

The regulators from the Federal and State ministries or departments are suppose to be preset on site at any field of activity in the mining industry. This will enable direct supervision, monitoring and control of the activity of all miners in the state.

The absence of regulators' presence at mining sites leads to the thriving of illegal mining activity at different unauthorized sites not only on the plateau but around the country.

There should be regulatory practices by the supervising government ministries and agencies to control:-

- Granting of mining licenses
- Opening of mining sites & claims

- Control of occupational hazards on mining sites
- Control of land degradation & environmental impact assessment
- Training of artisan miners on modern methods of mining and use of modern equipments.
- Close collaboration with miners association in the state.

When the supervising agencies does not participate in overseeing the activity of tin and columbite mining on the Plateau, it suffers serious neglect and as a consequence affects the industry as a whole.

7.4 Lack of collaboration and synergy with relevant association (Miners union);

There was an obvious disconnect between the practicing miners particularly the directors and the miners association. The directors are very wealthy and do not consider the activities of the mining associations relevant. There wasn't much restriction on their business therefore they do not see any need to stood low & beg or lobby for any favor through the association. Everything was moving smoothly for them therefore they don't see any need to attend union meetings. These actions of the mining company directors who know each other very well is inimical to the miners' union and invariably renders it irrelevant and unpopular. That is why so little is heard of the miners association despite the wealth of the practitioners or directors. Given a strong supported union the miners' association should have been one of the strongest in the country in terms of lobbying power.

CHAPTER 8:

8.0 PROPOSED REMEDIES TO REVIVE TIN & COLUMBITE MINING ON THE PLATEAU & NIGERIA

With my many years of experience in the solid mineral industry and as a way of suggestion. I felt that certain things must and should be put in place for the revival of this one great industry. For this great industry to regain its past glory many card must be put on deck. Did I hear some people say it's impossible in Nigeria? Nothing is impossible once the problem is known and there has never been a problem without solution. I know what this industry has done for me especially in my educational pursuit the employment it has provided me the confidence building and above all the professional reputation and discipline.

Permit me to digress a little, I remember vividly when a south – south delegate to the PRC said they had given a 5 years ultimatum to all states of the federation to generate and develop the natural endowment found in their domain because after five (5) years they will take full ownership of their oil resources and only remit certain percentage to the Federal government of Nigeria.

The issue above is coming in the heels of general clamor for restructuring in Nigeria and one of the subset for the agitation by one region is resource control.

The question here is wouldn't that be a blessing in disguise? If and when Nigeria is restructured, will the individual States having solid mineral endowment in their domain complain? Rather I believe and very much know that they will thank God over and over again. With the massive deposits, the capacity to transform economies and generate wealth, and the potential of solid minerals to attract mass foreign direct investment into these regions with favorable laws put in place and transform any weak economy into a strong global one. Then I should say these states should be in the front burner for the agitation. We are all aware of the moves by the south – south people to have a total ownership of their oil and probably that's what prompted the call for revival and the strong investment in agriculture by the northern states of Nigeria.   The following are personal suggestions proposed to revive the once glorious and noble endeavor based on the premise relied upon by the author which are decades of experience and direct involvement in the field not based on hearsay or interviews. Anchored on these facts and the need for immediate action the following remedial measures are postulated viz:-

8.1 The need for foreign direct investment in the mining sector.

Perhaps the best way to revitalize mining in Nigeria and also on the Plateau is to invite and attract foreign investors to the country and state by making friendly laws for both parties.   It is pertinent to say here that mining in whatever form is a huge and broad industry that is capital intensive. Massive capital investment in humans, machines and equipments are required to reactivate and sustain the solid mineral mining in Nigeria and Plateau State. This type of investments can only be sourced and accessed by opening wide the doors of Nigeria to foreign investors from all over the world. Initially, most foreign investors complained of unfriendly laws in existence regarding Nigeria's solid minerals sector. If not for these laws, they are ready at any time with global hard currency to pour into the country. Skilled man power and an update in technological advancement in the field of solid minerals mining are needed. These can be provided by foreign expertise that have the capability to do so. They only need to be inspired to the right place.

8.2 Private sector participation

As I have said earlier, the greater activity in the tin and columbite business is in the hands of private individuals. That is appreciated. The advanced capitalists' economies of the world have majority of their businesses in private hands. In Nigeria today, what is needed is more private participation. The industry can improve when many wealthy individuals and groups invest in the industry. We have so many well to do entrepreneurs who have capital but are contemplating the type of business to venture into. Such investors are welcome to the mining sector from any part of the world. More private sector participation is needed to revamp the mining industry and restore it to its former glory.

8.3 Plateau state and federal government involvement as Regulators.

The federal government and Plateau state governments should as a matter of urgency come to the rescue of the solid minerals industry. They can do it more than just mere rhetoric or pencil and paper thing.

There have been moves in the national assembly to enact legislation backing SOMPADEC (solid mineral producing areas Development commission) just as we have OMPADEC and others. This calling is wise in itself but it should go beyond the drawing board or the walls of classrooms. It should be a pragmatic move to restructure the solid mineral industry for the better.

The state government on its own part should in partnership with the relevant Federal government MDAs be proactive to invest massively through the appropriate ministry to revive solid mineral mining on the plateau. When that is done, it will complement the state government effort and serve as the principal internal revenue earner for the State through payment of taxes and royalties.

The federal and state governments, should concentrate more in the exaction stage of the solid minerals to give it a boost jus as the adage " a house without good foundation is as good as collapse" that is the assertion here. This is the area that had suffered oblivion which should have been the area that receives more attention. There can be no production into final product without raw materials. So therefore, government should invest in heavy excavation equipment and other relevant machineries. Government should also fully engage the Nigeria Mining Corporation (NMC) and lastly government should sponsor graduate miners on further courses and trips abroad to acquire sound practical knowledge in the field.

For better monitoring, the plateau state government should create solid mineral management board just like we have tourism corporation board and hospital management board to name but a few. This will go a long way in reviving the industry and managing it properly through sound administration. Government should organize workshops, exhibitions and field trips for miners to keep them up to date. Finally, both the state and federal governments should engage the service of consultant geologists to explore the vast potential solid mineral deposits yet untapped and at the same time prospect for other new minerals deposits deep in the earth's crust.

8.4 Training of Artisans and small scale miners.

Artisan miners most at times being referred to as illegal miners should be trained periodically in the basics of mining by the State or federal agencies free of charge to intimate them on the ethics, methods, concepts, dangers and benefits of mining. This is because they are citizens of Nigeria and deserve the right to gainful leaving as postulated for in the constitution of the Federal republic of Nigeria.   Since no matter how government monitor and regulate the industry, it cannot puff itself completely of this category of subsistence miners who must be there and are mostly the first to discover rich mines one way or the other whether at their backyards or a distance away at their farmlands which they indulge for survival. The training can be carried out through the industrial training fund (ITF) in collaboration with the Plateau State chambers of Industries, mines and Agriculture (PLACIMA).

8.5 The use of standard mining practices to check fraudsters.

Random and unauthorized mining practices have led to so many setbacks in the mining industry. Activities of fraudsters and crooks have led to the fall of prices in the country in the past. Coincidentally fluctuation of price is one of the most important characteristics of the mining industry not only for Nigeria alone but it is a global and unforeseen phenomena. These bad practices must be checked throughout the solid minerals mining hierarchy. Mining companies and tin sheds are springing up by the day throughout the State without authorization (approvals, licenses, or registration). This must be checked and curtailed by the supervisory and regulating body responsible for such. Additional legislation must be enacted in addition to the existing ones chiefly to regularize internal day to day running of mining activities in urban centers. The above mentioned legislation should be able to ensure consistency in pricing, uniformity in scale balance and weighing scale, occupational safety standard measures in mining sites including tin sheds and trenches. There should be compulsory use of steel armored helmets, nose protectors, coveralls and dust absorbers in all mining environments. Finally, there should be tin shed manuals for good manners placed at the entrance of every tin shed for good conducts. There should be good customer's service and sound public relation in the system. When all these are put in place and enforced through mining inspectorates, the ills in the industry will be brought to the barest minimum and finally eradicated.

8.6 Acquisition and use of high Tech mining equipments & modern methods of production.

To revive the industry and make it attractive to both local & foreign investors there must be conscience effort to modernize the industry and make it attractive to prospective investors. The types of machinery being introduced by the white miners since inception are really obsolete and in fact should belong to the museum. There are improved modernize digital operated machines which are satellite guided and robotic standardize. This type of high tech mining machines and equipments pride itself in high quality of resultant products and almost zero error. They give high return on investment because it gives 100% initial analyses, and predict the percentage of impurities in a given ore sample and suggests the best method of production to harvest the best quality and quantity.

Current global practice entails the use of modern and advanced digital operated machines and equipments to maximize production, reduce wastage, minimize health risk and occupational safety and reduce lost man hours. These mining machines and equipments come in variety, types and according to area of utilization. There must be strong will to invest large amount of funds to import the various machines and equipments available globally to use it to open the corridor of mining and as a way of diversion from black gold. There will be mass production both in quality and quantity for export because there is a constant demand for the product worldwide.

8.7 Partnering the miner's association.

The miners association which is the umbrella body for all miners in Nigeria with branch in Plateau State needs to collaborate hand in hand with the government regulators to advance the course of mining in Nigeria through favorable policies. Government needs to empower the association by granting them soft loan facilities sourced from Federal ministry of trade and investment so that they can disburse to their members to enable them to invest back into the mining business. The union should also be supported when they discipline erring members. Those mining directors who participate actively in the mining association and do not allow their millions to deceive them into believing that they are bigger than the association should be granted soft single digit loans and reduced tax wavers to enable them operate effectively without hitch. Government should also encourage these active directors by providing easy access to exporting facilities for their finished products. These facilities are in the form of transport cargo ships, port cranes and lifts, ports storage facilities, discounted custom duties and other incentives to encourage the miners and the country to produce to export rather than to consume and import. Finally, the wealth of most miners and the mining company owners and directors should be used as an advantage to form a strong lobbying group to pursue their interest through public and private circles purposefully for the sole aim of advancing solid minerals mining in Nigeria, Africa and the world.

8.8 Attitudinal change;

Through organized workshops and seminars the perception of most miners shall be influenced positively. The attitude of "getting rich quick syndrome" and "by all means" should be corrected while the unprofessional outlook and perception should be changed completely so that they can view and regard what they are doing as a profession and business endeavor rather than a provisional run–in-run-out thing. The prevailing thought of making fast money whether by good or by crook should be eroded and be replaced by trained and disciplined mindset.

This awareness should be carried out in all the mining companies, without any form of segregation in their class. This type of attitude is exhibited by the unskilled and less educated miners whose only goal is to sole the immediate problem. The training should be geared toward imbibing the culture of gradual and conscious move through the ladder of career progression to reach the peak and attain a status wordy of note. When this mobilization is fostered through propagation, it will right most of the wrongs in the solid minerals industry. Such mobilization should be co-sponsored by government and the private mining directors who are directly at the receiving end. The reform will make most miners to sit up and put their best seeing that they will not want to destroy their life long career in a day. Achievement in this policy direction will mean bringing sanity to the industry.

REFERENCE

1. Adams, H., 2001, Columbia Encyclopedia, Sixth Edition, available at www.bartleby.com.

2. Calvert, J.B., 2000, Tin 4, available at www.du.edu/~jcalvert/phys/tin.htm

3. Natasha, C., 2002, Tin mining of the Jos plateau, available at www.uni.edu/gai/nigeria/lessons/tin-mining.htm

4. Gibson, O., 2002, "Tin Smelting in Nigeria – the Challenge of our time." Proceedings of the 19th Annual Conference/AGM of the Nigerian Metallurgical Society, pp. 47 – 60.

5. Guanzhou, Q., Tao, J., Zhucheng H., Deqing, Z., and Xiaohui, F., 2002, "Characterization of Preparing Cold Bonded pellets for Direct Reduction using an Organic Binder." ISIJ International Journal, Vol. 4, pp. 20 – 25.

6. Kurt, M., 1980, Pelletizing of Iron Ore, Springer – Verlag Berlin Heidelberg, New York.

7. Rumpf, H., 1962, "The Strength of Granules and Agglomerates." Agglomeration (ed. W.A. Knepper), New York.

8. Tohidi, N., and Rames, V., 1997, "Preparation of Iron and Steel Burden." Seminar paper presented at Tehran University.

9. Kasai A., Murayama T., and Ono Y., 1993, "Measurement of Effective Thermal Conductivity of Coke." ISIJ International, Vol. 33, pp. 697 – 702.

10. UNCTAD (United Nations Conference on Trade and Development), (2007). World Investment Report 2007: Transnational Corporations, Extractive Industries and Development. New York and Geneva: United Nations.

11. Mahtani, D. (2008). The New Scramble for Africa's Resources. Financial Times Special Report, 28 Jan. 1-6.

12. Twerefou, D. K. (2009). Mineral Exploitation, Environmental Sustainability and Sustainable Development in EAC, SADC and ECOWAS Regions. *African Trade and Policy Centre Work in Progress*, 79. Economic Commission for Africa.

13. Morgan, P. G. (2002). Mineral title Management - the key to Attracting Foreign Mining Investment in Developing Countries? Trans. Instn Min. Metall. (Sect. B: Appl. earth sci.), B165-B170.

14. Girones, E. O., Pugachevsky, A. and Walser, G.

(2009). Mineral Rights Cadastre: Promoting
Transparent Access to Mineral Resources. Extractive
Industries for Development Series #4 June 2009.
Washington DC: The World Bank.

15. Obaje, N. (2009). *Geology and Mineral Resources of Nigeria*. London: Springer (Chapter 1).

16. Cowie, A. (2010): Tin, an Overlooked Commodity.
The Market Oracle, Aug 19, 2010
http://www.MarketOracle.co.uk

17. Davenport, J. (2010). Nigeria Aiming to Grow
Mining's GDP Contribution to 15% by 2015. Mining
Weekly, March 15, 2010.

18. Pastor, J. and Ogezi, A.E., 1986, New evidence of
cassiterite bearing Precambrian basement rocks of the
Jos Plateau, Nigeria – the Gurum case study,
Mineralium Deposita, Vol. 21, No. 1, pp 81-83.

19. McAllister, M., Scoble, M. & Veiga, M. (2001). Mining with Communities. *Nat. Res. Forum*, 25, 191-202. Morgan, P. G. (2002). Mineral title Management - the key to Attracting Foreign Mining Investment in Developing Countries? Trans. Instn Min. Metall. (Sect. B: Appl. earth sci.), B165-B170.

20. Metallic Minerals, October2, 2010. http://www.onlinenigeria.com/minerals/?blurb=517.

21. Funtua, I.I., Idris, Y., Oyewale, A.O., Umar, I.M. and Elegba, S.B., 1997, Determination of Tin in cassiterite ores and tailings by 241Am source X- ray Flourescence Spectrometry, Appl. Radiat. Isot. Vol. 48. No.1, pp 103-104.

22 . Evans, J.R. and Jackson, J.C., 1989, Determination of tin in silicate rocks by energy dispersive X-ray fluorescence spectrometry. X – Ray Spectrom. 18, pp 139.

23. Tin Investing News, September 30, 2010, Tin Advances on supply threats. http://tininvestingnews.com/483- tin-advances-on-supply-threats.html.